Amazon Echo

Master Your Amazon Echo;

User Guide and Manual

Andrew McKinnon

Legal Notice:

This book is copyright protected. This is only for personal use. You cannot amend, distribute, sell, use, quote or paraphrase any part or the content within this book without the consent of the author or copyright owner. Legal action will be pursued if this is breached.

Disclaimer Notice:

Please note the information contained within this document is for educational and entertainment purposes only. Every attempt has been made to provide accurate, up to date and reliable complete information. No warranties of any kind are expressed or implied. Readers acknowledge that the author is not engaging in the rendering of legal, financial, medical or professional advice.

Table of Contents

Andrew McKinnon

Introduction

Just a little over two decades ago, the idea of a cell phone itself was a distant dream, with only the most affluent masses being able to afford those bulky contraptions that they had to lug around.

Fast forward to a few short years later, and here we are today, where these things have become more of a necessity than a luxury, with new designs and software updates popping up left, right and center. And it is not just cell phones; technology has developed in leaps and bounds, what with smart phones, tablets and cloud computing and a whole array of scientific sounding terms that are actually easy to navigate in reality.

And behold, here is another one of those technological marvels that has been introduced to the world just a few short months ago – *Alexa*. Giving Microsoft's Cortana, Google Now, and the all-encompassing Apple's Siri a run for their money, Amazon has come up with a whole new voice-command device – the Amazon Echo – which they have fondly dubbed 'Alexa.'

Don't worry if you're not all that great at using technology-based devices. You don't have to be an expert. This guide will make it easy for you to understand and set up your Amazon Echo in no time. The Echo will help you and your family in a wide range of activities, answering various questions, keeping you on time, and basically acting as a personal assistant. And, Alexa is someone to talk to if you are home alone and are a little bored. The Amazon Echo comes with a lot of great features that make your life easier and more fun and this guide will help you get the most out of your Echo.

In the book, I have outlined the great features and benefits of using the Amazon Echo. I have also included some instructions on how to do certain things, recommended phrases for use and a few tips on how to control Amazon Echo the way you want to. As well as that, to finish off, I have included a list of Amazon Echo Easter eggs, a few fun questions for you to ask Alexa. You might just be shocked at some of the answers you get! This new product is going to start a wave of change for the future of technology and you are on the forefront. Learn now and do not be left behind; you picked a good time to start learning about the Echo! I hope it helps you make Alexa your own welcome home companion!

Andrew McKinnon

Chapter 1
What Is Amazon Echo?

Amazon Echo is a brand new device, in a brand new category. It looks like a speaker and, indeed, it is a speaker but it is also so much more. It's a speaker that you can talk to, a speaker that responds to your voice and does what you ask it to, within reason.

Echo, also known as Alexa after the software that Amazon has installed, is a small cylindrical unit, just 9.25 inches tall. It has no less than seven microphones, a 2-inch tweeter and a 2.5-inch subwoofer. It uses Far Field Technology, which means it can pick up your voice from another room and it can hear you over moderate noise levels.

Amazon Echo, let's call her Alexa, is an intelligent device. It is always on, listening, but contrary to some concerns; it isn't actually doing anything until it hears a certain word. That word is the "wake" word, and when Alexa hears it, she springs into life, ready to do your bidding. The default "wake" word is "Alexa," but it can be changed to anything you want it to be.

Alexa uses cloud-based processing and requires a Wi-Fi connection to work. The voices used by the device are lifelike, natural sounding and it uses NLP – natural language processing – algorithms that are built into the TTS – text to speak – engine, in order to produce a high level of accuracy.

Alexa offers numerous services – she will read the news to you, tell you the weather, play your favorite music and read you the sports headlines. She will give you up to date game scores for your favorite teams and tell you what the traffic is like on your route to work. She will read you a book, organize your To Do List and even write your shopping list for you, as well as keeping up with your calendar. And there is one smarter thing that Amazon Echo does – it integrates with SmartThings, Phillips Hue, Belkin WeMo and Wink to allow you to use voice control with home-connected devices. How cool is that?

Let's take a more detailed look at Amazon Echo and all the smart things she can do for you.

Andrew McKinnon

Chapter 2
Why Choose Amazon Echo?

The Echo is the first product Amazon has presented since the Kindle. Amazon doesn't simply want to be an e-commerce business, and that's why it has been trying to diversify its market. The Echo is a great product and has been successfully taking over the market in the past few months. It is one of Amazon's products that aim at making the customer's life easier with optimum services and easy functionality.

Are you someone who deals with a wide array of questions during your day and who needs quick answers to these questions? If you are, then you need not look any further. The Amazon Echo is the best tool you can get your hands on right now that can answer all your daily questions and perform many more operations. It can play your music, read you audiobooks, set alarms and much more. It's an amazing little device that can help you in many different areas of your life with just one word. Say the name, *Alexa* or *Amazon*, and you'll get your information. Sounds like "Open Sesame," doesn't it? Well, it really is that easy!

If you need a stylish and efficient personal assistant, Alexa is the one for you. It will solve most of your problems and will help you in your daily activities. Here are some of the many reasons why Alexa is an amazing voice-command device you should buy right now.

Easy to Access

The Amazon Echo comes with detailed and easy to follow instructions that help you set up your device. Managing your Echo is really simple and customer support is available at all times in case you cannot understand anything. You just need to choose the personal preferences and settings you need, and then you are ready to roll. The Echo will handle all your queries and assist you in whatever way you need.

Excellent Voice Quality

The voice quality on this gadget is simply brilliant. There's no other way to put it. If you've had a long day, Alexa can act as your music therapist, playing your favorite songs in excellent quality. The voice is crisp, loud, and has just the right kind of soothing pitch to make a long and tiring day feel good again with melodious music coming out of its speakers. So you can add stress busting to the list of things your Amazon Echo is capable of doing. Difficult days at the office don't seem so difficult now, do they? With Alexa, your life will be easier and less stressful.

Superior Voice Recognition

A frequent query people have is whether Alexa can differentiate between different human voices? It's a computer after all. How good can it be at detecting only your voice out of a thousand others? Well, you'll see just how good Alexa is once you start using her at home. She can easily pick out your voice among a crowd of voices, and retain it too! It's really impressive and surprising. Alexa is a really smart personal assistant. She can record what you say and then respond in whatever manner required. It also doesn't feel the need to constantly beep or talk to remind you of your notifications or anything. It remains silent and only speaks to you when commanded with the wake word.

Privacy Concerns

The Amazon Echo is very sensitive and can record almost everything in its vicinity when switched on. For reasons that are understandable, this feature is not something many people are fond of. Privacy concerns were obviously raised by people. But the peeps at Amazon were quick to address their worries. You see the Echo can only record when it is awake. It's always powered on, but it doesn't record anything unless you have spoken the wake word, *Alexa* or *Amazon*. Other than that, it will never record your personal conversations. And besides that, you can also delete unwanted recordings from the Echo later if you wish to. Just go to the "Manage my device" tab in the user profile where you can delete the unwanted recordings and keep things private. The people at Amazon take your privacy concerns seriously and you can rest assured that Alexa will keep your secrets faithfully.

Software Upgrades

Any technology can stay afloat in the market only by constant innovation and creativity. Just like Microsoft keeps launching new versions of Windows, or Apple keeps the iPhone up to date with the latest features by way of a new and better iOS coming out every few months or so, in the same way Amazon is also launching new and improved versions of their Echo operating system so that the device stays upgraded and users don't get bored. They are constantly adding more features and improving functionality. And the changes are not limited to just the structure. They have also added small but handy new features, like adding the wake word "Simon" to the device operating system. The software of the Echo is constantly upgraded, which makes sure you get to enjoy the latest features as and when they are released.

Natural Voices

Often, the problem observed with voice-command systems is that they don't completely understand what the user has said to them, or misunderstand the input completely. They confuse homophones, ask for repetitions, or process incorrect information. Alexa, however, is far ahead of its peers in this race. The device has a natural language processing system installed on it that is constructed on the text speech engine principle. In layman terms, this means that the processing systems on the Echo are highly efficient and can process your voice with far more ease and with greater vigilance than any of the others. Alexa will easily understand what you want to convey and will take appropriate action.

Cloud Processing

The Echo can hear everything happening around it and that includes all of the different voices that surround it at any moment. Even if it's something as subtle as the opening or closing of a door, the sound of your TV, or the bark of your dog, the Echo will capture it in the Amazon web service. Again, I must remind you that it only records when it is awake. A really nice feature the Amazon Echo has is that of cloud based processing. Besides operating the Echo directly, you can also control it by manual operation. This is done via the handy remote control provided with it or by voice activation. As the future of cloud computing seems to appear brighter and brighter, Alexa is a sound step ahead in this direction. It will store your data in the cloud without any commands. It's as easy as it sounds.

Hardware

The Echo is really a small wonder. It is a black cylinder, small enough to fit in any corner of your house without disturbing the surroundings, and large enough to tell anyone looking that it means business. It is powered by a DM3725 ARM Cortex-A8 processor and 256MB LPDDR1 RAM. These Texas Instruments processors give it the necessary processing speed and power to ensure a smooth delivery and voice quality. There are also 4 Gigabytes of storage space available on this device, which is more than enough to store the everyday recordings and other data. So you can see that Alexa comes with superior hardware to match her smart capabilities. It's really the best artificial assistant you can have.

Chapter 3
Alexa – Design and Setup

Dubbed with the working title 'Project D' or 'Doppler,' the scientists at Amazon have been working in their labs to unveil Alexa to the world for the past four years. Since bringing the revolutionary Kindle E-reader to the market, the Amazon Echo is the first gadget they have introduced, and it's simply wonderful.

So what *is* Alexa? Like Apple's Siri, Alexa is simply a voice command device, which works based on a question-answer system and controls smart devices around the house. It is meant to be a household product, consisting of a tall, cylindrical speaker and a remote control. And of course, there is the Amazon Echo app available which you will have to download onto your smart phone to operate Alexa. Alexa is wonderful and she is another step bringing us closer to something equivalent of Tony Stark's J.A.R.V.I.S.

How exactly does this work? The Echo contains a tiny array of seven microphones, with beam-forming technology that can pick up your voice from any direction. Echo is always on; it starts working, however, only when you use its code name – Alexa. If you don't like the name, you can change it back to Amazon. Amazon or Alexa, what the Echo does is use an on-device keyword spotting system to detect the '*wake word.*' Once the sleeping monster is awakened, it truly turns into a thing of power, lighting up and streaming audio to the cloud, collecting, storing and receiving information from Amazon Web Services that helps you with your questions and commands.

For the smart person who knows how to use the technology at their disposal, Alexa can prove to be the ultimate virtual companion. To begin with, even owning the Amazon Echo is a novelty in itself. There is a long process you will have to follow.

The first thing you need is an Amazon account, so create one or log into your existing account. Enter "Amazon Echo" into the search bar and click on the option that appears. The Echo is sold on an invite only basis so you will have to request an invite at the site. They will ask you for your details, following which your name will be added to a list of members who have also requested the Echo. After signing up, there is an interim period that follows, after which you will be given notice of the availability of your device. Amazon Prime members can buy it for a nominal fee though, once again, you will have to be chosen from the invite list to do so.

Design

When you receive the box with the Echo in it, here is what you will find:

- The Amazon Echo

- Power adapter to be plugged in
- The Amazon Echo remote-control, with an inbuilt microphone, music playback and volume controls
- The magnetic Amazon Echo remote-control holder, including an adhesive for sticking it onto non-magnetic surfaces
- Batteries for the remote
- A Quick Start Guide.

You are ready to go if you have each of these items. Activate your Echo by registering it on Amazon first. You can do this by logging into your Amazon account and start discovering the services available with the device.

Let's talk about the features and mechanisms that make Amazon Echo what it is, a superior voice-command device. It will help you to understand the entire basics of your device before you begin using it. The Amazon Echo is made up of various different components for voice recognition and data storage, along with the software, which creates a complex blend of technological prowess and usability. Be aware of these so you can expertly use it to the best of its capabilities.

The Amazon Echo is highly efficient at what it does, and this is possible only because of the resourceful and well-placed parts embedded in the device. This gadget is created to respond fast to your queries and provide you with accurate and quick results.

The Body

Standing at 9.25 inches and covering just over 3 inches of table space, the Amazon Echo is a really neat and stylish gadget, almost completely made of metal. It is cylindrical in shape, which ensures that it doesn't take up too much space. The tweeter is about 2 inches in width. The Echo also has a woofer that is about 2.5 inches in size, and is embedded in the bottom part of the device that is perforated. It is great for producing rich sounds, and it also has a reflex port.

Blue Light

Right at the top of the Echo, you will find two buttons – an on/off button for the microphone, and an Action button. There is a slim, translucent banner running around the edge of the circular perimeter of the Echo. This banner serves as a light ring that flares up when the speaker is on, and sits next to the array of seven microphones. The banner lights up in cyan color when the Echo wakes up, and that means it is ready to go. There are other colors too that the ring flashes, which signify different things. These will be explained later on in the book.

Microphones

The most important function of Echo is to recognize voices and respond to them. So being a voice-command device that has to respond to queries, the Amazon Echo obviously has to have good quality microphones because they are one of the most essential parts of the gadget. Echo is very efficient in doing what it does, and this is because it sports a circular array of seven microphones that are strategically placed in such a manner that they can capture sound from any direction. This gives the Echo the best response time yet. As soon as you say the activation word, also referred to as the *wake word*, the microphones pick it up and the Echo's light ring starts glowing cyan in color. This means that the device is active and can now be used.

Sensors

The sensors installed in the Echo help in the functioning of the microphones. They are made from beam forming technology, enabling it to pick up voices from greater distances than other similar products, and from almost any angle or direction. This makes the Echo much more home friendly as you can call out to it from anywhere in the house. The sensors also help connect to the Internet services when you request something of Alexa.

Remote Control

As mentioned before, the Echo comes packed with a remote control that goes hand-in-hand with it, and allows you to perform various actions well without the use of voice or with voice, if chosen. It is about 5 inches long, quite like the Amazon Fire TV remote control, and sports a rubberized grip for added comfort and hold. The best thing about the remote control is that it has a microphone built into it that allows you to directly talk to Alexa without having to shout loudly from across the room. Just press the button on top of the remote and you can use the microphone functionality. You can control the volume of your music or anything else you're playing through Alexa via the Echo app on your phone. You can also control the playback or other settings. The remote control comes with a magnetic holder, which is a pretty neat feature if you ask me. It allows the user to attach the controller wherever they need it to be. You no longer need to worry about having to carry it around the house with you.

Setup

We have taken a look at what the Echo looks like and what its components are. Now let's begin the setup of your Echo.

Setting up your Amazon Echo and getting it to work is very easy. Plug it in first, and then get your remote working by inserting the two AAA batteries you received along with the set in the box. The minute you insert the batteries the remote will automatically pair up with the Echo. If you are experiencing difficulty in pairing your remote up to the device, don't panic! First, download the Echo app and follow the instructions. The app is compatible with:

- Android phones and tablets (running Android 4.0 or above)
- iOS phones and tablets (running iOS 7.0 or above)
- Amazon Fire phones and tablets (running Fire OS 2.0 or above)

You can access it either through your usual app download center – Play Store, Apple Store – or via a Web browser.

Once you have the app, go to *Settings*, select your Amazon Echo, and then choose the *Pair Remote/Forget Remote* option.

Now that your device has been set up, connect your Echo to the home Wi-Fi network. Here is how you do it. Make sure your Echo is plugged into a power outlet, or it won't work. Before you connect it, remember, the Echo connects only to dual-band Wi-Fi, and doesn't support enterprise or ad-hoc networks. In other words, it is a device to be used at home, and not a company with Intranet.

After completing the setup, there are a couple of things you should check before you begin working. Give the device a name first off, so it can be identified. This also helps manage the settings of the Echo. Also, if you have multiple Echo devices in your home, giving it a name helps you recognize which device you are dealing with. To change the name of your Echo device, open the Echo app on your phone and go to *Settings*. At first, the device will appear with the name "Your Amazon Echo." Click on the name field, select the default name, delete it, and then type in whatever you want to name your Echo. After this, select the *Save Changes* tab and go back to your home screen. Now your Echo has a name of its own. You must remember, however, that this is only the name of your device, not the *wake word* for your device. For now, you can only set the *wake word* to Amazon, Alexa, or Simon. Changing your device name won't change the wake word. We shall discuss this later in the book. The device name is also what appears when you connect the Echo to Bluetooth, or any other network.

Open up your Echo app and go straight to *Settings*, and select the *Set up New Echo* option. On the Echo itself, press down and hold the Action button for five seconds. You will see that the circular light banner turns orange as your mobile device connects to the Echo and a list of

Wi-Fi networks that are available to you will appear on your app. Pick out yours and the choose *Connect.* If you cannot find your network, then choose *Add a Network* or *Rescan* to manually set it up. As soon as the network is connected, a confirmation message will pop up on the app, and you can return to the home screen.

Remember, Alexa also works on the concept of cloud computing, so you can access the Amazon Cloud via your Wi-Fi Internet. Follow the instructions through the app until your introductory video plays, giving you instructions on the basic voice commands you will need to get your own Alexa up and running.

Fun fact – unlike Apple or other devices, you don't need to set up your Cloud. It automatically connects when you hook your Echo up to your WiFi, making things far easier to navigate. Your data can be backed up on the cloud and can be accessed on the go from any device at any moment.

To make sure your device is connected to both the Wi-Fi and the Cloud; check the Power LED that is located above the power cord. It will light up in either case; if the light is a solid white color, you are good to go with your Amazon Echo connected to the WiFi and the Cloud with no hassle. If, however, the light is a solid orange color, you are in trouble, because your Echo is not connected to the Wi-Fi network. If the orange is a blinking light, then your Echo is connected to the Wi-Fi but not the Cloud.

Here is what you can do to fix this. Go back to the app and try reconnecting to your Wi-Fi network. Make sure you type in your password correctly. Needless to say, you should also check to see if your Internet is properly connected. Sometimes restarting your modem may help if the problem lies with the router and not the Echo itself. It could also be that the Echo is blocked by concrete material or walls, so try moving it closer to your router.

If you still have problems, try unplugging and re-plugging your Echo from its power source. Also check to see if you have registered your Echo to your Amazon account – this is absolutely essential if you want to get it up and running and use any of the facilities available to you. If you are registered, log into your Amazon account, and go to *Manage your Content and Devices*, pick *Your Devices* and look out for the name you have registered your Echo under. Deregister your device, and log out. Now try setting up the Echo again from scratch, and re-register.

If you are still having problems, contact Amazon Help and Support to get your Echo up and running without any problems.

Now we're on to the last activity for your Echo setup. You just have to key in a few personal specifications. This is to personalize your device, so that Alexa can get to know you and your preferences better. This will make her a better assistant. First of all, add the location of your Echo. To do this, once again, go to your Echo phone application and access S*ettings* on the navigation panel on the left side. There you'll see a *Device Location* tab. Select it and then enter the zip code of the area you are living in. If you see a zip code already present in the field, there's no need to do anything. This is because the Echo has a feature that enables it to automatically enter the zip code. This won't work for people living outside of the United States of America, though. So people living in other countries will have to specify the zip code or postal code manually. Whatever the case be, make sure the zip code/postal code you enter is correct, and if the zip code/postal code is already there in the field, make sure it is the right one. Afterwards, click on the *Save Changes* button and exit the page. This is your first step in personalizing Alexa. By letting Alexa know where you are living, you are allowing her to tune into all the local radio stations, get news about the local weather to you, and do other localized tasks for you.

Moving on, the second step in your way to personalizing your Amazon Echo is selecting the measuring system that suits you. You can choose between the Metric system and the Standard system for measuring distances, and between the Fahrenheit and Celsius for measuring the temperature. To alter these settings, access *Settings* on your phone app and pick what you want. This will save you considerable time, as you won't have to ask Alexa to convert the various measurement responses for you. She will just respond using your preferred system.

Now we're on to the Amazon account settings. Tackling this is easy. You are already familiar with registering your device on the Amazon website to gain access to all of the features and facilities provided by the Amazon ecosystem and to stay connected and updated. After getting your Amazon Echo device registered on Amazon, you can manage the account settings yourself from the phone Echo app, or you can even ask Alexa to do it all for you. It's that easy! Voice purchasing feature is the most important setting here, and this allows you to shop online with the help of Alexa. You can just give her simple commands and she will do the work for you.

In order to activate the Voice Purchasing feature, you need to go to *Settings* in the Echo app. There you can see a *Purchase by Voice* option. Click on it and it will prompt you to enter a confirmation code. This is a code you will have to enter each time you ask Alexa to purchase something for you. It is a four digit PIN. After you have entered this PIN, click on the *Save Changes* option and exit to the home screen. Keep in mind that this PIN is something you will be saying out loud many times whenever you make an online purchase with Alexa's help. This PIN shouldn't be something that's already a code for any other services or important accounts that you use. That would be dangerous for security reasons. The PIN you set up for Alexa will just act as a verification number before making any purchases online. Rest assured that your credit card and billing information is safe and won't be divulged in any way.

And that brings us to the next section of the account setup process, which is managing your 1-Click preferences. Anyone who is a regular Amazon user would be aware that after you enter your shipping address and mode of payment for the first time while placing an order, Amazon enables 1-Click ordering on your account. So, if you happen to order something on Amazon with the 1-Click ordering enabled, it will be automatically processed according to your details from the default settings that have been saved in your account. You can change the shipping address in 1-Click Settings under the tab named *Manage Addresses*. With Echo, you don't even need to set up any 1-Click order settings. Just set it all up once with Alexa and then she'll do all your shopping! You can update the 1-Click order settings in your account and include Echo in there, thus enabling Alexa to tap into the account settings and dig into the details of your order whenever you want to buy something from Amazon. You won't even need to enter any billing information this way and it will all be safe. All you will ever need to do is call out the verification PIN you set for Alexa, and that will be it. Enjoy your shopping experience!

Alexa has a really handy feature. Being the home device that she is, she has the ability to handle multiple user accounts. This means that more than one person can tie in their accounts together with Alexa. With Alexa, you can make a Household profile. This gives all the family members access to combined to-do lists, joint music libraries, and a lot of other features. You can even make joint purchases or use the account of your family on any other Amazon devices or accounts. To use this facility, just go to the *Settings* page on your Echo app and select the *Household Profiles* option. This will enable you to add a person to your Amazon Household. Just make sure that whomever you add to your Household account is actually present with you. The credentials and personal details of the person to be added will be needed when adding them to the Household. Follow the instructions in the app and enter the required information.

After doing this, save the settings and Alexa is ready to handle two user accounts. Only one account will run at a time though. To know which account is running at a specific moment, simply ask, "Alexa, which account is this?" and you will get the answer. If you need to switch to a different account, just command her to do so by saying, "Alexa, switch accounts." There are some common elements between the two user accounts: shopping and to-do lists. These can be viewed by anyone on the Household account registered to your Echo, and the people on the Household account will see any alterations within these fields.

If, at some point in the future, you feel the need to remove anyone from your Household in Echo, revisit the Household Profiles tab in the *Settings* menu on the Echo app and click on *Manage your Amazon*

Household. You will see the individuals added to the Household. Select one person you want to remove from the Household and click on the *Remove* option. To remove yourself from the Household, just click the *Leave* button and click on *Remove from Household* before you return to the main screen to finish the removal process.

Before you proceed any further, I would just like to remind you that any person who has been added to the Household Profile has access to your billing and credit card information. This information has been registered to your account, and by way of your Household Profile, is available to anyone else on the profile. This can be problematic to you. This is where the confirmation PIN comes to your rescue. If you are not comfortable sharing your credit card and billing information with anyone, or if you are worried anyone will make purchases on your credit card, all you have to do is keep the PIN to yourself. This will prevent Alexa from buying anything off the

Internet without your prior permission. Anyone else using Alexa won't be able to make any purchases.

This was the last step in the setup process. Now you are all set to start using your Echo device.

Chapter 4
Navigating the Echo and its App

Amazon prides itself in staying ahead of the competition, and this is why the Amazon Echo keeps getting continuous modifications and improvements. Customer feedback acts as an important tool while doing this, and Amazon is not one to diss customers. The software is constantly being updated, and new features are slowly being added. Here are some quick tips to work your way around the new Echo.

Amazon Echo Smartphone App

The Amazon Echo smartphone app is one of the most important parts of the whole system. Without it, the Amazon Echo device cannot function. We have already seen how absolutely indispensable the app is while setting up the Echo. All of the tasks given to the Echo are transferred to your smartphone first, and then processed by the phone and acted upon. As an example, if you asked Alexa to add something, say laundry, to your to-do list, this will first be sent to your smartphone. After the smartphone has processed it, an appropriate response will be framed for the command. Just like a smartphone, the Amazon Echo can also be paired with a tablet to enjoy the same benefits as that of a smartphone.

This makes it imperative for you to first get the Amazon Echo app on your smart device – either a phone or a tablet. When you download the Echo app to your smart device, please make sure that the device fulfills all of the earlier mentioned specifications. If your operating system is not compatible with the Echo, you may have to update it to the latest version to get the Echo app to work on your phone or tablet.

Once you have downloaded the app, install it onto the system. It doesn't have an overly busy looking interface. In fact, the app home screen looks pretty sparse with very little shown on the main screen, also called the home screen. All you can see there are the recent commands you have given to Alexa and the recent questions you have asked of her. However, if you take a look at the upper left corner, a small tab is visible which shows all the options available for your device.

In the Echo app, you can browse your to-do list, alarms, timers, and your shopping list. These are the things Alexa will keep tabs on. Then there's your music. Amazon Echo currently supports music from Amazon Prime, Pandora, Spotify, iTunes, iHeartRadio, and TuneIn. These are more than enough for a music lover to listen to their favorite songs anytime anywhere. The default mode for the Amazon Echo is Amazon Prime Music, but you can change it to any other service with your app settings. You can even create your own playlists.

All this could come off as a bit tiresome to some people, but trust me when I tell you that pairing your phone or tablet to the Echo is very easy and will give you much comfort in times of need. There is a lot of functionality tied in with the phone or tablet. Waking up your Echo device becomes much easier once you have it paired with your phone, or tablet. Not just that, specific settings can also be set on your smart device for receiving texts, looking for information, and resolving queries. Your smart device lets you operate Echo in a much easier and friendlier manner to your heart's content.

Watch out! The Amazon Echo is so user friendly and helpful that it can become an obsession for any user. Once you get used to living with Alexa, you'll get so dependent on her that you won't feel like leaving home without her being beside you. And perhaps this is the reason why Amazon is delving into newer and more portable gadgets that make it easier to take the Echo with you. People really are making Echo part of their lives, and the help that they receive from it is so unexplainable that they have really started to enjoy it. The Amazon Echo solves many of our everyday problems quickly, and offers many other benefits. The voice makes people get attached to it quickly. It almost adds a personal and human touch to the interactions.

Amazon Echo Pen

World, are you ready for even more awesomeness? Because the Amazon Echo isn't bound to stay on the top of your table or counter any longer. It now comes in the form of a small pen too!

Since the launching of the Amazon Echo in the market, many gadget lovers from all over the world have wanted to see it in a portable format, something they could take off their tabletops and carry with them. This is why the peeps over at Amazon created the Amazon Echo pen. It goes hand in hand with the Amazon Echo app, which is essential for its proper functioning. So now, people can enjoy the benefits of this amazing device even on the move.

You can write down your notes with the Echo pen with the assurance that this amazing piece of technology is available to assist you in any way possible. The Echo pen increases the possibilities of what you can do manifold. This multifunctional pen can store your interviews, record your lectures, and do much more. All you need to do is set up your Echo pen, and you can do all you want with point and play. The recordings can assist you when you are preparing for presentations or lectures, or even when you are just writing something.

The pen is really lightweight and slim, making it comfortable to hold and work with. And while maintaining all this, it still boasts 4 gigabytes of storage space, enough to record almost 800 hours of optimum quality audio. If that's not brilliant, I don't know what is? To establish connectivity with a computer you just directly connect it to the USB port on any laptop or desktop computer. These features make it the best helper for you during lectures and presentations. It is a must have for people who live in the moment and believe in staying ahead of time.

Activating your Echo with Voice Command

Let us now take a look at how to use the Amazon Echo using the very best of its talents.

While you can use the button on top of the Echo and the app to navigate the usage of the device, the Echo is, first and foremost, a voice command machine. Use Alexa to her full capacity – go on and wake her up by calling out her name. The minute you say *"Alexa"* the circular light banner will flare up and your Echo is now in action. When the Echo detects the 'wake' word, the light turns blue and starts processing what you say to it. It begins to send an audio stream to the Amazon Web Services that will answer your queries, and this audio stream will send even a fraction of a second of audio before the wake word. The audio stream closes once the Echo has processed your request.

How can you know if your command has been processed or not? To receive that confirmation, go straight to *Settings* in the Amazon Echo app, tap on the *Your Echo* option and go to *Sound Settings*. There, you can enable a '*wake up sound*' that is a short audible tone that dings every time the wake word is recognized. And if you want to know when the audio streaming has ended, select the '*end of request sound*' too, which will play once your request has been processed.

Now if you are not comfortable with the name and want to change '*Alexa*' for some reason – like having a family member in the house with the same name – you can change it to '*Amazon*' very easily. Once again, open up your app, go to *Settings*, select your Amazon Echo and choose the *Wake Word* option. There you can select '*Amazon*' instead of '*Alexa*' and the next time you call out Amazon, your Echo will light up, ready to respond to all your commands.

The voice recognition is excellent; a lot of customers feel that Alexa sounds far less robotic than Siri, and there are fewer instances of her misunderstanding you. The best feature about the Amazon Echo's voice recognition software is that it gets better over time by using your own voice recordings to improve its results. The Voice Services begins processing information – like your playlists – the minute your Echo turns on to improve response time and accuracy. There is also the Voice Training option that the Echo app provides, with which you can easily set up Alexa to understand and respond to you, as you would like her to.

Amazon also includes an incredible bookmark-sized list of all the things you can ask Alexa and expect her to answer without mistake. The topics are wide and varied – from alarm timings, to music playlists, to weather forecasts. Another fun feature of Alexa – she doesn't need much time to catch up! You can simply say, *"Alexa, what's the weather?"* and she will give you the forecast promptly.

Alexa also has her virtual fingers dipped into information pies like Wikipedia, so you can easily gain access to those databases – with *spoken information*, because, remember, Alexa is a speaker and a voice-command device.

What's interesting about the Echo is that it is essentially a device built to be helpful in the home environment. It doesn't have batteries and has to be plugged in if you want it to work at all, which means you cannot lug it around with you to parties and picnics, where there is no access to electricity. While many customers found this to be a hassle, Alexa is a very purpose-specific device, unlike the smart phone virtual helpers that are meant for at work. Alexa is like a toned-downed version of Richie Rich's robot maid; she can do everything from acting as an alarm clock, to waking you up, to helping you with your groceries.

Light Ring Status of your Echo

As I mentioned when I was describing the design of the Echo, there is a circular banner of translucent material that runs around the perimeter of the device. This is the light ring; we have already discussed how the color changes can be used to identify if the Echo is connected to the Wi-Fi or not. Other than that, there are a few more color codes that will help you handle your Amazon Echo better.

To repeat what I already said, when the Echo starts up, the light ring will flare up brightly with a solid, spinning cyan blue color. Before that, however, all lights are off – this does not mean that your Echo is switched off. It is simply awaiting your command, and will light up the moment you give the wake word.

When the solid cyan colored light starts pointing in your direction, it means that the Echo is busy processing your request. Essentially, this means that light will move in the direction of your voice no matter where you are situated, so you know whether your Echo is picking up your command or not.

The orange color code we have already discussed; when the spinning orange light flashes, it means Alexa is busy trying to sync to your Wi-Fi. However, here is something new – if the light turns violet, and begins to oscillate continuously, it means the Echo is having trouble connecting to the network. Follow the procedures mentioned above and try again to connect to your Wi-Fi.

If you turn the volume button on the Echo to the left or the right, you will be able to regulate the volume to your liking. When you do this, the light ring will turn a solid white color, indicating volume adjustment.

Apart from that volume button, the Microphone button next to it also affects this ring of light. If you turn it off, the band will emit a solid red light, indicating that it is off and it cannot pick up your voice via the perforations. You will have to press the button again to turn it on if you want Alexa to listen to what you command.

Voice Training

Alexa is very adaptive in nature. That's just how Amazon has built the device. The voice recognition software is really good and it keeps improving over time as it adapts to your voice. So before you start using Alexa full time, it would be great if you could do a bit of voice training. This will train Alexa to recognize your voice better and she will also match your speech patterns much more efficiently, giving you more accurate and quicker responses in turn.

Before we start the actual training, there are a few things that you need to be aware of. First of all, make sure the microphones on Echo are powered on; otherwise they won't pick up what you say. Secondly, don't use the remote control. The main motive of this voice training is to make Alexa accustomed to your voice so she can even understand you if your voice is coming from far away, or if it's muffled. That is the whole point of it, and the remote control completely defeats that purpose.

When you are ready to start your voice training with Alexa, open the Echo app on your phone or tablet, go to the navigation panel on the left, and select the *Voice Training* option there. Then click on the *Start* option. Now you're in Voice Training mode. The window on the app will prompt you to speak 25 different phrases. This will take a while. Don't stand too close to the Echo device when you're speaking these phrases. Just sit on your sofa or stand near the doorway. Be anywhere you assume you would usually be when talking to Echo. Speak in your normal everyday conversational voice. Don't go too slow, or too fast as this confuses the device. Be friendly and talk to Alexa as if you're talking to a buddy. This facilitates understanding.

During the whole process, if at any moment you feel like you have messed up a phrase, there's a way to instantly fix that. Just click on the *Pause* button on the screen, tap the *Repeat Phrase* option and you're good to go. Repeat the phrase you messed up earlier. There will be a *Next* button available after you are finished saying one phrase. This prompts you to the next phrase in the training program. You can also exit the training program halfway through. Just click on the *Pause* button on the screen and then select the *End Session* tab. This will exit the training mode. Alexa stores your progress in the training mode and doesn't make you repeat the phrases you've already said the next time you start voice training. She updates her system with whatever phrases you have already said. Alexa also doesn't record these Voice Training sessions to the Dialog History. So rest assured nobody will hear you sounding goofy.

Dialog History

As you are already aware, any conversations you have with the Amazon Echo are recorded in it. This helps the device improve on its response time and precision. So this obviously means that Alexa keeps transcripts of all your conversations with her in the storage memory. This is called the Dialog History, and the user can access it at any time. To access your transcripts, just open the *Settings* in the Echo smartphone app and click on the *Dialog History* option. This will open a window where all your interactions with Alexa will be displayed in list form, and you can choose whichever one you want to and listen to it. To listen to a recording, click the *Play* button you see near the transcript of the selected conversation. When you hit play, the recording starts playing.

There are two ways you can delete a particular conversation. You can either choose to delete the conversation and any record of it from both the device and the Amazon Cloud, or just remove the conversation from the device itself. If you want to delete a recording, just select that particular recording and tap on the *Delete* button lightly. Doing this will delete that interaction from both the device and the Amazon Cloud.

It won't be streamed anymore and all the Home Screen Cards associated with it will also disappear along with any data backed up to the Cloud. Be careful about this feature. If you only wish to delete the Home Screen Cards and keep the data backed up in the Amazon Cloud, just go to the home screen and click on the *Remove* button next to the transcript. This will hide the conversation from your view.

You can also delete all of your conversations with Alexa in one go. To do this, visit the *Settings* page on you Echo app and click on the *Manage your Content and Devices* icon. When you click on it, a window will appear showing you all your devices, and all the devices registered with your Amazon account. Select the Amazon Echo, click on the *Device Actions* menu as soon as the Amazon Echo window opens. It is a drop down menu, so from the *Device Actions* menu, click on the *Manage Voice Recordings* button. There you'll find an option to delete all of your conversations with Alexa. The *Delete all the Conversations* feature will completely wipe clean your recording memory. Every recording the Echo has ever created will be deleted from both the inbuilt storage memory and the Cloud storage of your Amazon account.

One thing that should be kept in mind before taking such a step is the purpose of these recordings. The Echo doesn't want to invade your privacy. It only records your conversations to constantly improve its own working so that it can satisfy you better. It has to constantly monitor and analyze these conversations to improve its response time and accuracy, because it operates on a self-correcting principle. Deleting these recordings will mean that the system will have no database to fall back upon, nothing to use as reference next time you ask it something. This will obviously affect the performance of the device. It will be like talking to a person for the first time.

Operating the Echo using the Remote-Control

Using the remote control is an alternative to speaking to your Amazon Echo. As we have already discussed, you will need to pair up your remote to the Echo to use it properly. Remember, at any given time, only one remote can be paired with an Echo. If you have lost yours and ordered a replacement, you will first have to get the new one paired up to the device.

To do that, open up your Echo app, and go to *Settings*. Select the name of your Echo and choose the option *Pair Remote/Forget Remote. Forget* the previous remote and pair up the new one so that you can begin using it.

Press and hold the button on the remote until you hear a small beeping sound. When you do, you know that it is ready to pick up your command. Continue to hold the button and speak your instruction into the remote; you do not need to use the wake word here because the remote, and by extension the Echo, will accept your command without it. Another advantage here is that you can use the remote when the microphones are muted, or when the noise is too loud for Alexa to process your voice normally.

You can also change the remote's start up beep, or completely get rid of it, if you want, by accessing the *Sounds Menu* from your *Settings* on your Echo app. I wouldn't recommend that, however – the sound is how you know that your device is transmitting and receiving properly.

Other than the main menu button, you have the audio playback buttons that will allow you to pause, play, stop, and adjust volume. Using the remote is essentially the same as speaking out your commands in that way.

Bluetooth

The app that you downloaded should look rather sparse, with little displayed on the home screen except the recent questions and commands you gave Alexa. There is a small tab on the upper-left corner that gives you all your options. You have your to-do list, your shopping list, alarms and timers you want the Echo to keep an eye on, and then your music. You are given access to Amazon Prime Music, iHeartRadio, TuneIn, iTunes, Pandora and Spotify. While it will default to Amazon Prime Music, you can select what you want in your setup and make your playlists.

Remember, the Echo is a speaker. Therefore, it can be easily used to play music not only via the various stores mentioned above, but also through Bluetooth. Sync your device to it and, like a traditional speaker, it will bellow out your favorite songs without any hassle. As always, turn your device on, with its Bluetooth set to pair, and placed in range of the Amazon Echo. Now speak to your Echo to get it in sync with the media device. You don't even need to spell it; simply say, *"Alexa/Amazon, pair."* Your Echo should respond with *"Ready to pair."* That is when you to go the Bluetooth settings on your mobile device and select the pair up option. It may take a few seconds for your device to read the Echo, so be patient.

If the attempt to pair has been successful, Alexa will respond with a *"Connected with Bluetooth."*

Now you are connected with Alexa over Bluetooth! Go ahead and stream all the songs you want and blare out the music loud! You can also connect via the Amazon Echo app instead of speaking to Alexa directly, though she will continue to give you the same responses as though you did speak to her. When you are done playing your songs, speak the command, *"Alexa/Amazon, disconnect."* And the Echo will automatically shut off Bluetooth and disconnect your mobile device.

An important thing to keep in mind while connecting Alexa to another device is that she can only read the music files present on the connected devices. This means that things like text messages and phone calls on a smart phone cannot be retrieved by Alexa's Bluetooth. Neither can videos, documents or any other type of files be sent, or received over Alexa's Bluetooth connection. The Bluetooth functionality on Alexa is just to listen to and control music and not anything else. You also cannot divert the audio signal it receives from a mobile device to a Bluetooth speaker or any other similar device.

The connectivity, however, is absolutely great in Alexa. Once you have connected and paired up a device to her, you can ease up and let it connect to the device anytime you want to listen to music. Alexa keeps track of all the devices it has been paired to, and easily connects to them when prompted from the device. So next time you want to connect to Alexa and listen to music, you don't need to go back to the *Settings* tab and do it all over again. Just switch on the Bluetooth on your mobile device and then connect it to Alexa. There will be no hassle and you will be listening to your favorite music in seconds.

Here is another great feature available on the Amazon Echo – you can control the music you are playing without touching the mobile device! Usually, when you connect over Bluetooth to a speaker, you will have to navigate pausing, resuming, stopping and the like on your device. Here, Alexa does it for you! All you have to do is get her to sync to your device, select the track you want her to play and let her navigate it! Use the following voice commands to keep your hands free while playing your tracks:

- Pause
- Play
- Stop
- Next
- Previous
- Restart

The creators of Amazon Echo have fondly decided to call this feature the Hands-Free Voice Control for Paired Devices. This helps you do your chores around the house without having to worry about touching your mobile device to control your music. The screens won't get dirty because you won't have to touch them at all. Alexa will do all you need to do on a single command!

Enjoy your Hands-Free Voice Control for Paired Devices! The only popular devices not supported by this feature are Mac OS X devices like the Macbook Air. This functionality will hopefully be added soon to the Amazon Echo.

Other Connected Home Devices

As I said before, Alexa is entirely a device that makes your home life easier. Did you know you could connect other home devices to her so that you can access them using your voice control? However, these devices are not many – Belkin and Philips – though there may be more added later. Right now, the device supports home devices for lighting and switches.

How to Connect Your Devices to Amazon Echo

Before you can even get started with this, you will need to:

- Download the companion app for the device you wish to connect
- Use that app to set up the home device
- Make sure all the software for the connected home device is up to date.

Some devices will need to be connected through a hub, like a SmartThings or Wink hub. To do this:

- Open the Alexa app

- Tap on **Settings**

- Locate **Device Links** menu and tap on **Link With ...** Choose the name of the service you want to link with

- A login page will appear on screen for the third party service – login with your details and follow the onscreen instructions to finish the setup

- Once you have done this, you can go ahead and connect your entire device to Amazon Echo.

To get your Echo connected to these devices just follow these steps. First download the manufacturer's companion app on your mobile device and then set it up so that it can be connected to the Echo. Either command Alexa with the voice instruction, *"Alexa/Amazon, discover my devices,"* or use the Echo app to navigate *Settings* and go to *Connected Home Devices* and select the *Add new Devices* option. If the Echo discovers the device it will respond with, *"Discovery is complete. In total, you have *** reachable home devices under this Echo."* If it is unable to find it, it will say, *"Discovery is complete. I couldn't find any devices."*

If the device cannot be reached, it will appear as *Unreachable* in the app. If it has been connected, that will also pop up on the app and then you can control it with your voice. You can tell Alexa to switch your lights on and off and she will do it! You can even create a group of Home Devices that you can control at once. Go to *Connected Devices* under *Settings* on your app, and simply create a Group and add all the devices you would like. Now you can turn on, adjust the brightness and turn off all the lights in your house without flipping the switch!

Music Services

Alexa can now play music not just via Bluetooth but also from various online music services. You can choose from a rich array of music services to play on your Amazon Echo, be it iTunes, Spotify or iHeartRadio. You can play music from any of these services and more just with a word of command. To listen to music from supported music services, first off make sure that the version of Echo app installed on your smartphone or tablet is the latest version available. If you don't have the latest version, you can get it by following some easy steps. In your mobile device, open the app store and look for "Amazon Echo." Click on the official Amazon Echo app in the search results and check which version you have currently installed on your device. If there is an *Update* option available in the window, click on it and download the latest update so you can utilize all of

Echo's latest capabilities. Don't worry if you don't see any option for update. This only means that you already have the latest version of the Echo app installed on your mobile device. Once your app is up to date, you can enjoy all of Echo's music services!

All the music you have in your Amazon Music Library can be accessed once you set up your Amazon account and sync it with your Echo device. If you don't have a subscription to Amazon Music, get one as soon as possible, because it's a great online music library service which allows you to access a wide range of genre and artists at a really reasonable cost. You can also go for Amazon Prime Music, which is also a great way for members to enjoy millions and millions of songs for free. Your Amazon Prime Music can also be synced with your Echo device, and can be played back any time. If you don't want a Prime Music subscription, however, that's fine too. The Amazon Music Library works pretty much the same way with your Echo device, allowing you to upload as many as 250 songs to your online library from a computer for free. If you get an annual subscription to Amazon Music, you can also increase this limit to 250,000 songs! How great is that?

How to Import Your Own Music Library

What if you have tons of music stored on your computer that you want to play though? Perhaps music that you have downloaded from another place. That's easy enough to do. As I said before, you can upload as many as 250 songs for free and here's how to do it:

- Open your Amazon Music Library and sign in. You must do this from the computer where the music is actually stored.

- Go to the menu on the left and click on **Upload your Music.** If you have not already done this, you might need to download the Amazon Music Importer – you will be prompted to do so. Just follow the on-screen instructions.

- Once that has been done, click on **Start Scan**. This will run an automatic scan of your computer to see what music is stored in your iTunes library, if you have one, and in your Windows Media Player libraries. You can also choose to manually browse your computer for music but that can take some time to complete.

- When the Amazon Music Importer has found all your music, you can either click on **Import All** and all of your tracks will be added to your Amazon Music Library, or you can choose **Select Music** and pick certain tracks to be added.

Playing your music with Alexa is really simple. Just make sure she is plugged in and connected to your account, and then tell her to play any particular song. All it takes is a simple command, "Alexa, play the song (name)," and she will look up that particular song in your music library and promptly play it back for you. Sometimes, the song might not be in your song library. In this case, when Alexa is unable to locate the song you asked for in your music library, she will go on to look for the song in Amazon Prime Music library, and further

Digital Music Store. She will check with the samples in there and if the song is available to you, Alexa will play the song.

If you don't feel like asking Alexa to play the music for you, you can also do this by the smartphone Echo app. Just open the app and click on the *Your Music Library* option in the left navigation panel. Then you can either search for the song manually in the search bar, or you can tap into your library by clicking on the *Songs* tab and then looking for the song you want to play. You can look for *Artists, Genres and Albums* in much the same manner. And you can do the same by asking Alexa to do it.

If you want to use music services other than the ones provided by Amazon, say TuneIn or Spotify, you have to link up your respective accounts to your Echo first. For this, you have to use the Echo smartphone app. Open it up and go to the *Settings* tab. There you will find an option named *Music Services*. Click on it and you will find a list telling you the names of all the music services that can be readily connected to the Echo device. Select the service that you want to use with Echo, and a window will appear, prompting you to fill in your account details. Do this and Alexa will sync your accounts with the device. Now you are good to access any music available in these accounts.

The music on these accounts can even be played on the Echo without linking the accounts to the device. That is a really nice feature. But if you don't link the accounts to Alexa, you won't be able to use certain features like creating a custom station in iHeartRadio. If you want to have access to these features, just link those accounts to your Echo. When you are finished linking up all your music services accounts to your Amazon Echo device, you can play your favorite music on Alexa to your heart's content. Go on and create your own custom radio stations in iHeartRadio or Pandora, tune in to any popular station with a command, and access podcasts, programs and much more with ease!

You can do the smallest of things with Amazon Echo that you would be able to do on a computer when using your music services. There's even a like/dislike feature you can use. If you want to like or dislike a song, just command Alexa to do it. Say, "Alexa, thumbs up/down" while the song is being played, and she will do as you command. Alternatively, you can spell it out for her by saying "Alexa, I like/don't like this song," and she will like/dislike the song accordingly. If you don't want to use the voice-command feature and wish to do this with the Echo app instead, just open the app and click on the *Now Playing* tab in the app. To bring out the current list of songs playing, click on the *Queue* option. Then choose the song that you want to like or dislike, and you'll see thumbs *up* and *thumbs down* icon there. Select the appropriate one and you're done.

Some of the music services that you use, like Pandora and the Amazon Prime stations, allow you to take out a track that is being played too often and remove it from the rotation, as you might already be familiar with it.

You can use this feature with Alexa's help too. Command her by saying "Alexa, I am tired of this song," and the track will be removed from your selection of songs by her. As with any other feature, you really don't need to spell out the exact thing you want her to do. She is smart, and understands your mood. So she picks up your cues and does what you want her to do without you having to spell it out concretely. The same goes for the Echo app. You can do this by going to the app and clicking on the *Queue* option in the *Now Playing* tab. Select the track you want to remove from rotation, and tap the *I'm tired of this track* button. This will remove it from your playlist.

Other than these advanced features, you have all your regular features that you can use with the help of Alexa. Things like adjusting the volume, stopping or restarting the song, pausing or resuming the song, looping or shuffling tracks can be done with simple commands. Alexa will also provide you with all the information available about the track you are listening to, like the song name, the artist, the associated album, release date, and any other auxiliary details. You can just call out her name and ask her to do this for you. This is fully functional in the Amazon music services, but third-party music services might not support it, as they are restrictive of certain features and don't permit you to do or know certain things. As an example, let's consider TuneIn, iHeartRadio, and Pandora. They don't allow you to loop the playlist and if you want to listen to the songs over again, you have to do this manually. Similarly, some of the music services do not allow you to restart a track you are listening to, and some don't let you switch to the next or the previous track.

Amazon: Shopping for Music

If you like a particular song, you can tell Alexa to buy that song for you. You can do this as you are listening to it on any of the numerous Amazon Echo radio stations! You can also do it by asking for a song directly. All you have to do is tell Alexa the song name, artist, or album. Following this, Alexa will look for your song through the samples in Digital Store, and then you can buy the song without any trouble. The 1-Click mode helps make the payment even faster!

The Voice Purchasing feature must be enabled in your account for you to be able to purchase music off the Internet. We have already covered the steps required to set up your Voice Purchasing, so you can go ahead and jump to the next step: making sure all your 1-Click payment details are accurate and up to date. If you already have that taken care of too, then you are ready to begin shopping for songs. If you want to buy a song that you are currently listening to, just tell Alexa to buy it by saying, "Alexa, buy this song/album." She will buy it for you. If you want to buy something else, just tell Echo, "Alexa, shop for this artist/album/song (name)." To verify your purchase you will be prompted to say your Voice Purchasing PIN once, and when you provide it, the money will be debited from your account and the song will be added to your library.

To purchase music from the Amazon Digital Store you have to be aware of a few things though. If you are using an Amazon Gift Card to purchase the music, then it is necessary for you to be physically present in the United States of America to be able to do this. If you are paying for it, then a United States billing address is required, and any one of the United States banks must issue your mode of payment. Without fulfilling these preconditions, you will not be able to buy music from the Digital Store.

As of now, the "Complete This Album" feature is not available in the Amazon Echo, but is expected to be added soon. Pre-ordering and MP3 Cart feature are also unavailable currently. But one benefit of buying music from the Amazon Digital Store is that the Amazon Music Library won't add it against your storage limit in the library. It will be stored there for free, always. So your Echo can download or play it at any time with great ease!

Besides all of the above mentioned facilities, your music purchases can also be accessed from a different account. We have already discussed the Household Profile feature. This allows you to use the money from your family's account to buy the songs or albums, in case you do not have sufficient balance in your personal account, or don't want to use it to make payment then music can be bought from the Digital Store through any of the user accounts registered under the Household Profile. The steps for purchasing are exactly the same as mentioned earlier. When you are done, Alexa will ask you which account you wish you use to make the payment. There you can select the appropriate account. If you happen to have chosen an incorrect account, you can cancel the transaction by quickly saying "Alexa, cancel!" This will make Alexa cancel the purchase. Then you can proceed to switch accounts by commanding her, "Alexa, switch accounts." Once the accounts are switched, you can place the order again, and buy the music you want. Do take note that you must know the Voice Purchasing PIN in order to make payments from someone else's account.

Note: There is no need to panic if at some instance you happen to forget the Voice Purchasing PIN you entered into your Amazon Echo. You can easily reset this PIN. For this, open the Echo app and click on *Settings*. Select the *Voice Purchasing* tab and there you will be allowed to enter a new verification code for Voice Purchasing. Key in the new code, click on *Save Changes*, and you are good to go. The verification PIN has just been reset. You can now proceed to buy anything you want from the Internet.

Chapter 5
Some Practical Applications of Alexa

Using Alexa to help you around the house certainly makes things easier! She can be a multi-purpose assistant; from to-do lists to alarms, she can manage it all.

Set Alarm and Timer

To use the alarm facility on your Echo, simply give Alexa the command. You don't even have to spell it out; just tell her, "*Alexa, wake me up at (time),*" and she will set the alarm for that particular time! Another added advantage is the fact that the alarm will still go off even if you mute the Echo and the light ring is red. Alexa is a determined assistant – she *will* get you to work on time!

You can snooze her of course, by saying, *"Alexa, snooze."* She will go silent for exactly nine minutes before blaring loudly to get you up and running again.

Remember though, the alarm does not reset itself automatically. You can also set the alarm only 24 fours earlier. If you tell a friend a week in advance that you want him/her to wake up on this day at this time, chances are they will forget. Alexa is much like a person, which is why you can set the alarm only one day in advance.

The Timer works in much the same way. Prior to 24 hours, you can set it to go off by giving the voice command. You can either specify the time you want it to go off, or mention the number of hours instead; either way, Alexa will accept the command. She will also tell you how much time is left on the timer if you ask her. However, you will have to use the app to pause the timer.

Ask questions – collecting information

Did you know that Alexa could tell you a joke? Or if you would like, she can read to you information from Wikipedia or convert the dollar into pounds. She can even tell you how to spell a word, give you the background information of an actor or spew general trivia on anything you would like.

All you have to do is command her. The Amazon Echo will connect you to the Internet and you have your own assistant doing the research for you. If, for instance, you want to know details about a famous actor, you just need to say, *"Alexa, tell me about (actor's name)."* The Echo will respond to you, and if it is a website like Wikipedia you want to access, it will read out the information for your convenience.

If you have the zip code/postal code set up in the Echo app, you can even access the weather. You can learn the forecast for up to seven days, and ask for the weather in any part of the world. Once again, just ask Alexa and she will answer you. The weather is updated on a half-hourly basis using Accuweather. Some of the voice commands that you can use are as follows. For the purposes of this, we are using "Alexa" as the "wake" word:

To ask what the current weather is for your locale, say "Alexa, what's the weather?"

To hear what the future forecast is, say "Alexa, what's the weather for the weekend?" or "Alexa, what's the weather for this week?" or pick a specific day and say "Alexa, what's the weather for ...?"

To hear the weather for another city, say "Alexa, what's the weather like in ...?"

And, to check your own forecast for rain, say, "Alexa, will it rain tomorrow?"

You can even get Traffic Information! Set your starting point and your destination in the Amazon Echo app.

Alexa will tell you the best route to take and predict your ETA too. Of course, you will have taken her along with you if you want her to direct you; so long as she is plugged into your car, she can easily give you traffic updates whenever you ask her.

How to Set your Travel Information

- Open the Alexa app and go to the left navigation panel

- Click on **Settings**

- Choose **Traffic**

- Where it says **From** and **To**, click to input the addresses

- Click on **Save Changes**

You can add in one stop on your route, to do this, click on **New Stop** and input the details.

To ask Alexa to give you a traffic update for your route, say:

- "Alexa, how is the traffic?"

- "Alexa, what's my commute?"

- "Alexa, what's the traffic like now?"

Manage your shopping and to-do lists

Remember when we discussed the Echo app? The shopping and to-do lists are the very first things you see when you download it. You can use that to manage your groceries and your routine for the day!

You can add, edit, review and remove items on these lists. Alexa will respond to all commands as long as you instruct her to. To print the lists, however, you will have to use the desktop app instead of the Echo. You can also use the app to search Amazon or Bing for a particular item on your shopping list!

You are able to see up to 100 items on either list and you can view your lists in the Alexa app even if your mobile device is not connected to the internet. That means you can check your shopping list when you get to the store or, if you access the Alexa app from your computer, you can print off the lists. Here are some of the ways you can add to your shopping and To Do lists using the app or voice control:

To Do This	Say This	Use the Alexa App
Add items to either the shopping or To Do list	"Alexa, add ... to my shopping list" "Alexa, I need to buy ..." "Alexa, I need to ..." "Alexa, put ... on my to do list"	Open the shopping or To Do list from the left navigation panel, type in the item name and click on +
Review your To Do or Shopping lists	"Alexa, what's on my shopping list?" "Alexa, what's on my To Do list?"	Open the shopping or To-Do list from the navigation panel
Edit items on your lists	N/A	Open the lists, select the item you want to edit and type in the changes. Click on **Save**
Remove an item from a list	N/A	Select the appropriate list and locate the item you want to remove. Click on the down arrow beside it and click on **Delete Item**. Alternatively, tap the checkbox beside the item and click on **Delete**
View tasks that are complete	N/A	Open the list you want to look at and click on **View Completed**. If you want to remove all the complete items, click on **Delete All**

Print a Shopping or To Do list	N/A	You will need to use the Alexa app from your desktop computer web browser for this. Select the list you want to print from the left navigation panel and click on **Print -** top right corner
Search Bing or Amazon for a Shopping list item	N/A	Open the shopping list and select the item you want to search for. Click on **Search Amazon for** or on **Search Bing for**

Read Audiobooks

One of the latest features to be added to the Amazon Echo is the ability to read audiobooks. That's right, now Alexa can read your books, too. Sweet!

The integration and support of other devices and ability to handle different file types was missing from the Amazon Echo in its early stages, but Amazon has been stepping up its game recently. They have added some cool new features to make Alexa more user friendly, and one of them is the Read Audiobooks feature. Now, the Amazon Echo's speaker won't just be limited to playing the limited media stored in your online libraries, i.e. Amazon Music, Amazon Prime, Spotify, TuneIn, iHeartRadio and others. The Bluetooth pairing functionality lets you use Echo as a Bluetooth speaker. This means that any media you have on your phone can be played back to you on Echo by connecting it via Bluetooth. So if you have audiobooks stored in your smartphone, go on and listen to them in Alexa's voice as you relax in your living room.

For doing this, you just need to set up your Echo device as a Bluetooth speaker first. And this is no hassle. It can be done with a simple voice command. You have to say, "Alexa, pair Bluetooth," and she'll instantly start giving you instructions on how to pair your phone to her. You have to go to the Bluetooth settings in your tablet or smartphone, and pair it with the device named Alexa. Once this is done, you can enjoy the audio you play on your phone being played through Echo.

There's only one little limitation to this. You cannot control the playback with voice commands. This means that if you need to play, pause, seek, or switch any tracks, you will have to do it on your phone. You can't command Alexa to do that for you. But hopefully, Alexa will be able to manage these voice commands on her own too in the future. The firmware is constantly being upgraded with amazing improvements being done.

Amazon Echo, or Alexa, is a voice-activated assistant in a way, and thus, her abilities need to be constantly evolved and extended. Amazon has recently added the Audible support to it, making it able to read audiobooks. If you own an Audible account and have eBooks in your library, just connect Alexa to it and you can listen to the books. All you need to say is the name of the book. "Alexa, play the audiobook Harry Potter." Audible has made the download of two audiobooks from their libraries free for Amazon Echo users to celebrate this joyful event. Just download the Audible app and you can use this feature.

Here are the steps to be followed to read audiobooks:

1. To start any audiobook you own in your Audible library, say, "Alexa, read (name of audiobook)."

2. If you want to resume a book you were reading earlier, just do it by saying, "Alexa, read my book."

3. Playback can be controlled by using the commands, "Alexa, go back" and "Alexa, go forward."

It's as simple as that. There are many other audio playback devices that can read your eBooks for you, like Chromecast and Roku. But they have interfaces that have to control by display. Amazon Echo, on the other hand, is a novelty. It brings freshness to the idea because it is voice-controlled, and makes our lives much easier in that way.

Use Echo to Order Items

You can use Amazon Echo to order items that you previously ordered through Amazon. To place your order, simply say "Alexa, reorder ..." And name the item you want to re-order. If the item can be purchased, Alexa will tell you the name of the product, the price and, in the Alexa app, you will be shown some more information about the item. If you want to order the item just say "yes".

Echo will place an order using your Amazon account details for payment and shipping. These orders are covered by the same free shipping policy as orders made through the website on a computer.

You can also make changes to the ordering system through the Alexa app. For example, you can switch off voice purchasing altogether, or you can set up/change the voice PIN code that you have to use when making a purchase. This just adds a layer of security to your account to stop accidental purchases, or to stop someone else from using your account.

As a reminder, to do this:

- Open the Alexa app

- Go to the left navigation panel and select **Settings**

- Choose whether you want to deactivate/activate voice purchasing or set up a PIN code from the options given.

Should the item you want to reorder not be in stock, or no longer be available, Echo may give you some alternatives from Amazon's Choice. This is a system that picks out products that are rated highly, and competitively priced with Prime shipping. This won't happen all the time – if an alternative can't be found, the item you are looking for will be added to your shopping list instead.

Before you can do this, you must have:

- Either a 30-day free trial or a yearly subscription to Amazon Prime

- An Amazon.com account

- A US billing method and address.

Here are some of the commands you can use:

To order a specific item, say "Alexa, reorder ..." and name the item. The response you get will depend on a number of scenarios:

When	Echo will say
Echo finds that there is a previous order for the item	**If you don't have a confirmation code:** "...The order total is $... Should I order it?" **If you did create a code** "...The order total is $... To order it, tell your voice PIN code."
No previous order is found but an alternative from Amazon's Choice is recommended	"I didn't find that in your order history but Amazon's choice for ... is ... The order total is $... Shall I order it?"
No previous order is found and no alternative is found in Amazon's Choice	"I didn't find that in your past orders so I have added ... to your shopping list."
The item is no longer an Amazon-Eligible item	"I found ... but I can only reorder Prime-Eligible products. See your Alexa app for options."

The item is out of stock	"I found ... but it is temporarily out of stock. See your Alexa app for options."
It is eligible for Prime shipping but it is an Add-On item	"I found ... But cannot order Add-On items over Echo. See your Alexa app for options."
You try to place an order using an account that does not have Prime membership	"I found ... But can only reorder products for Prime members. See Alexa app for options."
You try to place an order but there is an issue with the file billing address on your account	"Sorry, but there is a problem with the billing address on your account. Please visit Amazon.com to complete your order."

Link Amazon Echo with Your Calendar

Amazon Echo is able to look at your calendar and tell you what is coming up. This will also work with any calendar that has been shared with you. To begin, you have to link your Google Account and Amazon Echo together, using the Alexa app. Anyone else in your household with a Google calendar can also link theirs as well.

Note: be aware that events on your Google Calendar that is linked with Echo are available for anyone who interacts with your device. To link your calendar, follow these instructions:

- Open Alexa app

- Go to the left navigation panel and choose **Settings**

- Then select **Calendar**

- Click on **Link Google Calendar Account**

- Input the login details for your Google account and then follow the on-screen instructions to give Echo access.

To Manage Your Calendars

- Open Alexa app

- Go to the left navigation panel and click on **Settings**

- Click on **Calendar**

- Check the boxes beside the calendars that Echo can read out to you.

Questions you can ask Alexa about events on your calendar are:

- "Alexa, when is my next event?"

- "Alexa, what's on my calendar?"

- "Alexa, what's on [name of other person]'s calendar?"

- "Alexa, what's on my calendar tomorrow at 9 p.m.?"

- "Alexa, what's on my calendar Saturday?"

Chapter 6
Amazon Echo Tips and Tricks

As well as all of the above that Echo can do for you, there are a number of little tips that you might want to know about.

1. Stop Echo From Listening For the Wake Word

Amazon Echo may always be listening but it does not mean that it is doing anything. In fact, Alexa will not wake up until she hears the "wake" word. However, sometimes you might want to be able to talk freely without worrying about whether Alexa is going to wake up or not. So you need to stop her from listening for that magic word. This is a simple case of pressing on the mute button that is on top of the device. When you press it, a red ring is highlighted and Alexa goes quiet until you press the button again.

2. Force Amazon Echo To Update its Software

Just like most other digital hardware, Amazon Echo contains a CPU and that means it needs software to run. Amazon confirms that Alexa will search for any updates available every night but, what if you need to see if there is an update before then? Perhaps something isn't working right and an update will solve the problem.

Back to that trusty little mute button again – just hit the button and leave Echo on mute for at least half an hour. Turn it back on and you have your update.

3. How to Use the Web to Access Amazon Echo

When you first set up Echo you must do it using the mobile app. This is mainly so that your Wi-Fi can be picked up and set up. However, you can also use the web on a desktop computer to get into quite a few of the settings for Echo, as well as accessing your shopping and To Do lists. Just go to http://echo.amazon

4. Linking Family Prime Accounts to Echo

You can also do this from the web page. Open up **Settings** and scroll down. Locate the option for setting up your Household. It is really helpful if all of the people being linked are members of Amazon Prime, or at least share a Prime membership. The shared member that you are adding also needs to download the Alexa app on to their mobile device and has to agree to join the household.

5. Using a Different Amazon Account to Control Echo

If you wanted to use another person's Amazon account on Echo, you can do so quite easily. They just have to be a part of your household. It might be that all the music is in one account and all your downloaded movies and books are in another. To find out which profile is currently being used on Echo, say "Alexa, which profile am I using?" If you want to switch to a different profile, say "Alexa, switch profile" and the next one in the list will be loaded. If you want to go to a specific profile, say "Alexa, switch to ...'s profile."

6. Using One Amazon Account To Control Different Devices

Each profile recognizes certain devices that are connected to Echo, those devices set up using the profile. If you wanted to, you could set up profile groups. For example, you could have one called "Desk Lights" and have it control two or three specific lamps. You need to set up a group and a group name for each profile.

If you can't remember to call the "lights" and keep saying "desk lamps" instead, you can set up two groups that control the same devices, each one with a different name. And two profiles can each use the exact same names for their groups but have each group operate different devices.

7. How to Annoy Your Family

Because Amazon Echo works on Far Field technology and because you can use a voice-controlled remote with it, you can have some fun! Go into another room and leave your kids in the same room that Echo is in. Now say, through the remote control, "Alexa, Simon Says..." And follow it up with the command you want. You could ask her to tell the kids to turn the TV off, or that it is bedtime. If you are trying to annoy adults and you want Echo to swear, all that will happen is you will get a beep in place of the swear word.

8. Do Some Simple Math with Echo

Echo is very good at simple mathematics. For example, you can say "Alexa, add two and five" or "Alexa, what is three plus eight?" Echo will also understand floating point values, commonly known as decimal points. So you can ask it math questions that have decimal points in and she will be able to calculate the answer for you.

9. Making Amazon Echo Repeat an Answer

If you didn't hear the answer to your question, you can ask Alexa to repeat it. Just say, "Alexa, can you repeat that?" and you will get the answer again. Just saying, "repeat that" doesn't work particularly well so it just goes to show that a little politeness goes a long way, even with a digital assistant!

10. Ask Amazon Echo to Calculate Dates for you

Echo is also perfectly capable of handling basic date calculations. You can ask her to calculate how many days there are between two specific dates. All you need to do is say "Alexa, how many days until ...?" And add in the date; you will get a correct answer. She will also understand public holidays, such as Easter, Hallowe'en and Christmas.

11.   How to Talk to A Real Live Person

There really are real human beings whom you can talk to if you have any issues with Echo. Just go to http://echo.amazon.com/#help/call and input your phone number. You will get a call back from someone who seems to know exactly what they are talking about and should be able to help you solve your problem.

12.   Amazon Easter Eggs

There are loads of Easter eggs in Amazon Echo; you just need to know where to find them all! The following list has been tested out and all of them work. Go ahead, ask Alexa any of these questions and see what kind of answer you get back! Some you may recognise from popular films.

- Alexa, I am your father.

- Alexa, who lives in a pineapple under the sea?

- Alexa, what is the loneliest number?

- Alexa, how many roads must a man walk down?

- Alexa, all your base are belong to us.

- Alexa, how much is that doggie in the window?

- Alexa, Romeo, Romeo wherefore art thou Romeo?

- Alexa, define rock, paper, scissors, lizard, Spock.

- Alexa, beam me up.

- Alexa, how much wood can a woodchuck chuck if a woodchuck could chuck wood?

- Alexa, define supercalifragilisticexpialidocious.

- Alexa, who's your daddy?

- Alexa, Earl Grey. Hot. (or Tea. Earl Grey. Hot.)

- Alexa, what is the meaning of life?

- Alexa, what does the Earth weigh?

- Alexa, when is the end of the world?

- Alexa, is there a Santa?

- Alexa, make me a sandwich.

- Alexa, what is the best tablet?

- Alexa, what is your favorite color?

- Alexa, what is your quest?

- Alexa, who won best actor Oscar in 1973?

- Alexa, what is the airspeed velocity of an unladen swallow?

- Alexa, where do babies come from?

- Alexa, do you have a boyfriend?

- Alexa, which comes first: the chicken or the egg?

- Alexa, may the force be with you.

- Alexa, do aliens exist?

- Alexa, how many licks does it take to get to the center of a tootsie pop?

- Alexa, what are you going to do today?

- Alexa, where do you live?

- Alexa, do you want to build a snowman?

- Alexa, do you really want to hurt me?

- Alexa, what is love?

- Alexa, who is the real slim shady?

- Alexa, who let the dogs out?

- Alexa, open the pod bay doors.

- Alexa, surely you can't be serious.

- Alexa, to be or not to be.

- Alexa, who is the fairest of them all?

- Alexa, who loves ya baby?

- Alexa, who you gonna call?

- Alexa, who is the walrus?

- Alexa, do you have any brothers or sisters?

- Alexa, do you know the muffin man?

- Alexa, how much do you weigh?

- Alexa, how tall are you?

- Alexa, where are you from?

- Alexa, do you want to fight?

- Alexa, do you want to play a game?

- Alexa, I think you're funny.

- Alexa, where in the world is Carmen Sandiego?

- Alexa, where's Waldo?

- Alexa, do you know the way to San Jose?

- Alexa, where have all the flowers gone?

- Alexa, what's in a name?

- Alexa, what does the fox say? (ask a few times, you will get multiple answers)

- Alexa, when am I going to die?

- Alexa, I want the truth!

- Alexa, make me breakfast.

- Alexa, why did the chicken cross the road?

- Alexa, where are my keys? (ask the question twice)

- Alexa, can you give me some money? (ask the question twice)

- Alexa, knock knock.

- Alexa, what are you wearing?

- Alexa, party time!

- Alexa, party on, Wayne.

- Alexa, is the cake a lie?

- Alexa, how do I get rid of a dead body?

- Alexa, are you sky net?

- Alexa, your mother was a hamster.

- Alexa, set phasers to kill.

- Alexa, roll a die.

- Alexa, random number between "x" and "y".

- Alexa, random fact.

- Alexa, tell me a joke.

- Alexa, heads or tails?

- Alexa, mac or pc?

- Alexa, show me the money.

- Alexa, what is the sound of one hand clapping?

- Alexa, give me a hug.

- Alexa, are you lying?

- Alexa, my name is Inigo Montoya.

- Alexa, how many angels can dance on the head of a pin? (there are 3 answers to this one)

- Alexa, see you later alligator.

Andrew McKinnon

Chapter 7
Some FAQs

So we have gone through all the workings, purposes and possible uses of the amazing device that is Amazon Echo. However, there might still be some queries or doubts that you need cleared up, and this is why I have written this section. If you have any concerns or doubts about your product, then below is a list of answers that will hopefully resolve those issues. Users and potential buyers frequently ask these questions, and the aim of answering these questions is to bring the user closer to the device and be able to use it in a more effective manner without running into any issues. Some information might seem repetitive, but it's important for novice users. In case your query is not answered here, you can find an abundance of information online regarding your Amazon Echo, and you can even contact the Amazon Helpdesk. They are always ready to help you resolve any problems.

1. Can Voice Purchasing be turned off in Echo?

Yes, Voice Purchasing *can* be switched off. It is really easy to do so. Just open you Echo app on your smartphone or tablet and go to the *Settings* page. Then click on *Voice Purchasing* and turn it off. Save the changes before exiting and you're good. Besides this, you can also enter a verification code for Voice Purchasing that Alexa will ask for every time someone tries to make a purchase through your account.

2. How do I purchase music on Echo?

Purchasing music on your Amazon Echo device is supremely easy. It takes no time, especially if you have 1-Click payment enabled. Just place an order and Echo will use the default payment settings of your account while doing so. Alexa can also read you back the product details if you want, and you can use a confirmation code while making voice purchasing to add security to your transactions.

3. What happens to deleted Voice Recordings?

Echo is really smart in what it does, so it provides you with two options when you want to delete the voice recordings. You can delete them from your device while still being able to keep a backup on the Amazon Cloud, or if you want them gone for good, you can delete them both from the Cloud and the device. Echo will just remove the date and the Home Screen Cards associated with the recordings when you decide to delete them. But if you delete just the Home Screen Card, Echo will keep the recording and will only remove the Home Screen Card. The recording will be safe. Individual recordings can also be viewed and edited in your device by going to *Settings* in your smartphone app. You can check them in the History section, and delete them if so required.

4. Can all of my Voice Recordings be deleted at once?

Yes, you can easily delete all of the voice recordings done by Echo in one go. To do this, just log in to our Amazon account that is associated with your Echo device, and go to www.amazon.com/myx. On the page that shows up, click on Amazon Echo and do it yourself, or contact the Customer Support service. You can play all of your recordings from your account, in the same way as you do on your phone. The deletion request can take a while to be processed. Remember that Alexa keeps record of your conversations with her for a reason. It is not to breach your privacy but to make her help you in better ways. She adapts to your way of speaking by listening to the conversations and evolving accordingly. Deleting all the recordings at once can affect her performance and she may start responding differently once you are done. So make sure you use this feature carefully. Your recordings are always safe in your Amazon Cloud account. If need be, individual recordings can be deleted in your Dialog History on the smartphone app.

5. How to delete individual Voice Recordings?

You just have to open the Echo app on your smartphone or tablet and go to the *Settings* tab. From there, click on *Dialog History* and you can see a list of all the voice recordings Echo has stored. Listen to any of them and delete any specific recording as you wish. Just tap on the little *Delete* button beside the entry to do so.

6. How do I review what I have asked my Echo?

Your voice interactions with Echo can be reviewed anytime. This can be done simply by going to the *Dialog History* tab in the *Settings* page of your Amazon Echo smartphone app. Alexa groups all your interactions into two categories: questions and requests. Just tap a request if you want to know more details about it. By tapping the play button, you can also hear what was uploaded to the Cloud for that entry. Some interactions can be incomplete. This happens when Alexa doesn't understand you fully and hence, cannot keep a complete record of what you said. To help improve her response, you can provide feedback on wrong or incomplete translations by going to the History settings.

7. How does Alexa identify the wake word?

Amazon Echo is designed to be a device of the future, an assistant that can predict and understand your needs. It only acts when addressed. And this is done by the wake word. The device employs a keyword spotting technology to recognize the wake word whenever it is spoken. This technology is built into the device. Since the device is powered on all the time, it can detect the wake word any time, even when it isn't active. Just when it detects that a wake word has been spoken, it starts streaming audio to the Amazon Cloud, beginning from a second before the wake word was spoken.

8. Can the microphones on Echo be turned off?

Yes, indeed. Although the seven microphones on the Amazon Echo are always active as a default setting, you can change these settings and turn them off as and when required. There are two buttons present on the top of the cylindrical device, one of them being the microphone button. Just press it to toggle it on or off. The light ring around the top will tell you about the status of microphones. When the lights are a mild cyan color, this means that the microphones are active and working properly. On the other hand, a red light on the ring indicates that the microphones are currently turned off. This means that the device will not respond to any requests and won't be activated when you say the wake word until you turn the microphones back on. Regardless of that, however, requests can still be made to Echo by using your remote control, as it has a microphone built into it.

9. How do I ensure my voice is streaming to the Amazon Cloud?

When the Echo is activated by the wake word, by pressing the button on top of the device, or by talking into the remote controller by holding the *Talk* button, the light ring on top of the device turns cyan in color. This indicates that the Echo is active now and is streaming all your audio to the Amazon Cloud. This is how any request or question you ask Alexa is processed. The audio starts streaming as soon as the wake word is detected by the device, and stops when Alexa has processed your query. If you cannot always see the light ring to make sure the audio is being streamed, you can make things easier for yourself by activating the *Wakeup Sound* feature on your Echo. Go to the *Sound Settings* on your Echo app and enable the *Wake up sound* option. This makes the Echo play a short audible sound every time it wakes up. The same feature can also be applied at the end of streaming so that it lets you know when Echo is done streaming your audio. It is quite a useful feature if you are sitting in a different room.

10. Will the Echo perform better with time?

That's a definitive yes. The voice services in Amazon Echo are designed to capable of evolving and improving over time. The more it listens to and the more it processes, the better it gets at understanding the user. The Echo keeps voice recordings in store for this very reason. These voice recordings serve as reference and also provide context when the Echo is looking for results to your questions. This gives you improved results over time. As soon as the Echo is activated, the device starts to process lots of information including your music playlists, your podcasts, and other data, to improve its precision and response time while answering your queries. This can further be improved if you provide Alexa with feedback. To provide feedback, just visit the *Dialog History* tab in the *Settings* menu in your Echo app, and use the Voice Training function to train Alexa to understand you better.

11. How do I wake up Alexa?

This can be done in several different ways. The easiest way is to just say the wake word (Alexa, Amazon or Simon, or whatever you want to set it to) out loud while the microphones are switched on. You can also do this by clicking the button on top of the device that activates it, or alternatively, you can press and hold the talk button on the remote controller and speak into it to wake the device.

Conclusion

There is something about Alexa that is infinitely more approachable than a cold, impersonal smart phone. Perhaps it is her name itself, which is more homely than Siri or Cortona. Perhaps it is the fact that she can convert kitchen measurements for you without issues. Perhaps it is the fact that Alexa has been intended to be a home companion, unlike other mature voice assistants that offer a wider range of features.

Whatever the reason, the Amazon Echo —Alexa — is your ideal home assistant who can offer you help whenever you need it. She is easy to use, easy to navigate and not very high maintenance; the only downside is that she cannot be moved from her power source, and a number of her applications are limited to the Amazon ecosystem alone.

However, for someone familiar with Amazon's systems, she is a joy to use, with incredible voice recognition software that rarely goes wrong. And since she is meant to be used, as a home device anyway, the lack of a battery is a less of a bother than you would expect.

I hope this book helped you find your own Alexa and get her to work for you! I want to thank you for downloading it and, if you found it useful, interesting or just a little bit fun, please consider leaving a review for me at Amazon.com. This doesn't just help me; it also helps other readers to decide that they want to buy my book.

Good luck!